Sundown

poems by

Ed Gold

Finishing Line Press
Georgetown, Kentucky

Sundown

ACKNOWLEDGMENTS

*I am happy to thank the following journals and magazines for publishing earlier
versions of these poems:*

Charleston Currents, If, Then
Cimarron Review, At Hebrew School
Cyclamens and Swords, Crossword Puzzle
Front Street Trolley, Saturday Morning
In These Times, SOS
Kakalak, Ark, Fugue for the First Grandchild, Neruda's Questions
Kansas Quarterly, Waiting for Amy in Front of the TV
Masters Poker League Poker Poems (UK), Texas Hold 'em
New Verse News, Why, Just Stay Calm
New York Quarterly, Valentine
Passager, Loveship
Petigru Review, Heads or Tails
Poetry Now, Heaven of Cowboys
Puerto del Sol, An Owl, or my Brother, Victimized
Rat's Ass Review, Signals
Star 82, Woke Up This Morning
The Ekphrastic Review, The Next People
Think, Dewdrop
Washington Dossier, Montego Bay, Jamaica
Window Cat Press, ZXCVBNM

Publisher: Leah Huete de Maines
Editor: Christen Kincaid
Cover Art: Amy Robinson
Author Photo: Amy Robinson
Cover Design: Elizabeth Maines McCleavy

Order online: www.finishinglinepress.com
also available on amazon.com

Author inquiries and mail orders:
Finishing Line Press
PO Box 1626
Georgetown, Kentucky 40324
USA

Table of Contents

for Amy

At Hebrew School

1

On the first page of my book,
Abraham walks with his son
into a blessed sunset.
From a balloon, he sings in pencil,
"Love is a many splendored thing."
Eighth notes float in the sky,
mingling with the Jewish birds.
The guy next to me says
our teacher is a homo.
So this is Hebrew School.

2

The guy next to me is now drawing
on his Hebrew Alphabet Card.
A dog lifts his leg
to pee a broken line
on the doorpost of the Hay.
A naked woman lies down
in the curl of the Mem.
Just hanging on
to the foot of the Gimel,
Santa Claus cries for help
in English.

3

On every other page,
magic.
Sticks turn into snakes,
an ocean splits,
people fall into pits
and lose their coats
and have to wrestle angels.

Or this: a bush on fire
and not one leaf crisps
or curls or twists away.
On the next page,
everyone forgets
to be astonished.

Saturday Morning

Behind the backs of the congregants,
attentive in their pews,
we dangled David Hoffman's brother down
from the front row of the balcony,
lowered him to the clock.
The rabbi paused.

When we lifted Mark up by his ankles
and gathered him in among us,
the rabbi spoke on ascension,
patience, and not losing one's hold
on one's family
in the general falling down of things.

I suppose it would have been a catastrophe
if David Hoffman's brother had slipped from us
into the laps of the Dachmans or Danzanskys
during the responsive reading, the adoration,
or the silent prayer, but we didn't care.

How much longer could we endure
the pits of our bellies,
yearning toward lunch?
How much longer could we breathe
in the clench of the tie,
the pinch of the good shoe?

For centuries, the Jewish People have suffered
at the hands of God, Men, and Microbes.
In the gradual constriction of our throats and toes,
we have endured the eternal sermons.
We wish to run in the street in our tennis shoes.
We have David Hoffman's brother by the ankles.
If your sermon isn't over in thirty seconds,
We Will Release Him.

An Owl, or My Brother, Victimized

1

He tried to hide
under my coat with me,
but they caught him
anyway.

They put masking tape
over his mouth,
hemming in the owl there
so he couldn't talk.

He sent this note.

2

"Why, yes, officer, we got a note
from his teacher just yesterday."

3/4/56

Dear Mrs. Gold,

Arthur scribbled while we were
drawing. Then he drew an eye
in the mess and claimed he
had done an owl. Now really!

Mrs. Pigeon

3

OK Really.
Nothing good happened
in school today.
We had to make masks.
Boo.
Yeah sure, real scary.

"What else?"

Nothing. (He had seen it,
and he wasn't talking.)

4 (what he had seen)

THE NUMERALS
lined up
gigantic
in front of the water fountain

The Grades
moving regularly
away

signs of a scuffle
feathers all around

5 Exhibit E

Your honor, the owl
in question
is essential to my case,
my star witness:
he must testify.

Grant us time.
Grant that the defense
will find it.

6 I take the stand

"Where were you
during the time in question?"

Inside,
where I was sick
of having to use
dotted lines
to draw the angels.

7 The Summation

So when the gang grabbed Arthur,
they didn't know they also had the owl
(because it was in him).

They didn't know that I had them
caught in my coat, which I was wearing,
where they were running catching taping etc.

They will do time
in the hoosegow
for these mistakes.

Valentine

I am over 18 years of age
Yes I want to know how to
get girls through hypnotism

I have checked the box
next to the words

I have enclosed my
please rush me my

Waiting for Amy in Front of the TV

You are cashmere bouquet,
oil of olay,
dove, joy.

I am bird's eye, deep blue,
wheat and rice and corn chex
over you.

I wish we had nine lives
of suds and spin and tumble dry
in a gentle heat,

my pears, my sunkist,
my luckiest of all
lucky strikes.

SOS

And these are the generations of Post:

And the Lord spoke unto Post,
commanding him to minister
unto the health of the Lord's people.
And Post retired into his white barn
and caused to be created
a drink he named Postum
and two cereals he called
Grape Nuts and Elijuh's Manna.
But a great hue and cry rose up
among the God-fearing people,
and Post changed Elijuh's Manna
to Post Toasties.
And it came to pass
that 40% Bran Flakes was born
in the white barn,
and soon became the most chosen
from among all the breakfast foods
in the world,
and the profits were manifold
that the Lord caused to descend
upon his servant, Post.

And Post begat Marjorie,
who married Edward Hutton.
Into their fold,
they gathered Jell-o,
Swans Down,
Minute Tapioca,
Franklin Baker Chocolate,
Walter Baker Coconut,
Calumet, La France,
and Maxwell House.

And the Posts prospered
and soon came to be called
General Foods.

And during the great depression,
General Foods acquired
the patents of Clarence Birdseye,
and of Rosellius for Sanka,
and Kool Aid, with cyclamates,
and SOS,
and duly begat Shake 'n' Bake,
Cool Whip and Tang,
Maxim and Brim,
and purchased Burger Chef
for the health of the Lord's people,
and today is number one in bubble gum
in all the world
and first in ice cream in Brazil.

Woke up this morning

on the wrong side of the bed,
in the wrong bed,
wrong part of town.
wrong town.

May a helicopter
yank me up out of here
and drop me down
on the right side

of the right bed
by you.
Stay put:
I will find you.

If I get there and
you are out searching for me,
I will have no idea
where to begin looking for you.

Ansonborough

Today, Isaiah,
the descendant of a slave,
is painting our porch ceiling,
sprucing up the pale blue
to fool the haints.

For years, the haints have not been fooled.
They snicker at the dinge and float right in,
but by tomorrow, the spirits of the dead
will look up and see blue water,
which, it is said, they cannot pass through.

Isaiah takes one last hit off his joint,
stands up from the railing,
puts on his plastic mask,
and reaches up to spray
DCL012 Gullah Blue.

Go somewhere else,
we tell the haints
and the man who paints,
whose mother grew up down the street
but can't afford to live here now.

Ark

I don't know what possessed us
to eat the doves.

We were so drunk,
and you were wearing that green dress.

It wasn't like we didn't have
a boatload of other choices:

two of everything that wasn't extinct
for god's sake, but no,

we had to have those delicious,
delicious doves.

Since then,
we have floated blind,

hoping we bump up against land
before we devour everything.

Why

after the murders at Emanuel A.M.E., Charleston, South Carolina

We asked the red bottle-brushes blooming off the back porch,
we asked the woman who was singing and writing parking tickets,
we asked the colossal white blossoms of the magnolia tree,
we asked the cashier named Wilnetta at the Harris Teeter,
we asked the cedar waxwings swarming the holly berries,
we asked the new baby, Helena Wren Silverman,
we asked the hailstones striking west of the Ashley,
we asked the oil truck that overturned and blocked I-26,
we asked the helicopter circling the neighborhood,

we asked the couple holding hands under a maroon umbrella,
we asked the two mourning doves sitting close on the wire,
we asked the cardinal who placed a millet seed in his mate's mouth,
we asked the aviator sunglasses forgotten on the porch table,
we asked the smudgy smoke of the citronella candle,
we asked the blue flowers on the Kleenex box,
we asked the juice glass with a decal from a moose hall,
we asked the first brown clutch of leaves in the green of the pin oak,
we asked the empty hammock on the porch next door,

we asked the crow we thought was an eagle until he cawed,
we asked the green anole who hopped on a branch and turned brown,
we asked the hawks whose chick refused to leave the nest,
we asked the loquat tree that didn't blossom and fruit this year,
we asked the mutant sunflowers sprouting under the bird feeders,
we asked our neighbor whose throat is healing from radiation,
we asked the house finch on the sconce with his eye crusted over,
we asked the little boy who played dead under the pew,
we asked the mockingbird who sang for five minutes before starting over.

The Warnings that Came with the Chair

We did not ignore all the warnings:
we did not stand on the chair, and
we did not use it as a stepladder.

But I must admit we did not check the bolts
every three months and retighten them.
We don't even know where the bolts are.

We never examined the chair
for a missing, damaged, or worn part,
and we didn't stop using the chair

until the part was replaced
by a new part,
which only the manufacturer could supply.

And while I was sitting in the chair,
I asked you to sit on the armrest,
hoping you would say yes.

We were so lucky:
serious injury could have occurred
because it clearly states

that the chair is designed
for only one person,
and once you accepted my invitation

and sat down,
we soon were both on the chair
and in it,

exceeding the safety capacity
by a factor of two,
exposing us to a range of risks.

We were lucky to survive
our failure to heed
the printed warnings.

Nursery Rhyme

It astonishes my daughter
how stupid I am.

For example, I am Daddy McStupid
for suggesting "fleece" when she sings:

"Mary had a little lamb
at least as white as snow."

"Okay, okay," I give in.
""If not whiter."

Dewdrop, let me cleanse in your sweet brief water these dark hands
for Billy Glasner

*cento of haikus by Basho, Kikaku, Shiki, Issa,
Shusan Kato, and Onitsura*

Darting dragon-fly, pull off its shiny wings and look—bright, red
   pepper pod.
All the time I pray to Buddha, I keep on killing mosquitoes.
I want to sleep—swat the flies softly, please.

I kill an ant and realize my three children are watching.
After killing a spider, how lonely I feel in the cold of night.
For you fleas, too, the nights must be long, the nights must be lonely.

Where there are humans, there are flies and Buddhas.
Don't kill that fly—look, it's wringing its hands, wringing its feet.
Dirty bathwater, where can I pour you—insects singing in the grass.

Autumn cicada, flat on his back, chirps his last song.
Even with insects, some can sing, some can't.
Insects on a bough floating downriver, still singing.

Signals

blink twice
if you love me
but have been afraid to say

blink twice
if you are carrying
a concealed weapon

blink twice
if the red X of the sniper
has found us

blink twice
if doctors put tiny cameras
in your brain while you slept

blink twice
if the lord put the fossils in the ground
to test your faith

blink twice
if you are reading this poem
against your will

blink twice
if you want me
to rescue you

Crossword Puzzle

In the southeast quadrant,
I thought the answer was intuits,
but intuits turned out to be insults,
joining Iowa with Wessex,
which meant the southeast corner was done,
leaving only the heart open.

Then the Neva ran through St. Petersburg,
Linear B was the ancient Minoan language
not yet deciphered,
and a bass sax led to x-ray eyes.

But when Linear B turned out be A,
I learned that the Latin word for lover
is amateur,
and that solved a very difficult puzzle.

The Next People

after Linda Fantuzzo, Mythic Realm, 2019

The last thing we did was paint the ceiling green.
We had put it off forever.
Then you walked out the door into the busy light,
and I climbed up the gleaming ladder
and closed the window.

Above the empty fireplace,
we left the rainforest painting
we bought in Costa Rica.
Neither of us could imagine
looking at it in another room.

We left the door open for the sun to paint
a door of dappled light on the shiny floor
for the next people who will fill
this hollow space,
hoping for a different ending.

Texas Hold 'em
for Ivy and David Berney

The hardest thing
is to get away from
a gorgeous loser,

but after the flop,
if you don't hit,
you gotta drop.

Say goodnight
to that pocket pair,
that ace-king suited.

Don't kid yourself:
you have nothing.
Get out before it gets expensive.

You flash me
the pretty cards
you dropped with.

What do you want me to say:
that you aren't so stupid
after all?

I know: you had it won at the turn
and lost it on the river.
Wah wah wah.

Listen, until you see the river,
you don't even know
what you have.

I know how you feel.
I've released so many dazzling losers
into the muck.

Loveship

That eye-bite you flashed me,
was it an amoret or a blench?
Are you my half-marrow,
or are you just foading me?

I am mally of your fernticles and murfles.
I swingle in the crisples of your hair.
I linger at your heart-spoon,
the soft curve of your nuddle.

Let's shab out to the sky parlor
under the dream hole
and smick together and snoozle
and quaggle all over like jelly.

Don't be carked:
there will be no afterclap.
I am no mere belly-friend or franion,
no wowf performing murlimews.

We are side by side
in the kissing crust,
and it smells like
cloves and oranges.

Just Stay Calm
a cento-haibun

It's going to be just fine. We are doing an incredible job.
Everything is under control. It's just one guy coming in from
China. We do have a plan, and we think it will be handled
very well. That's a pretty good job we've done! I said it would
go away, and it will go away. Looks like by April, you know, in
theory, when it gets a little warmer, it miraculously goes away.
Stock market starting to look very good to me! The flu is worse!
Just stay calm, it will go away. One day, it's like a miracle. It will
disappear. We have handled it very well. I'm choosing not to
wear a mask. It's only a recommendation; it's voluntary. So when
we have a lot of cases, I don't look at that as a bad thing. I look
at that, as in some respects, a good thing because it means our
testing is much better. Really, it's a badge of honor. This is the
democrats' new hoax! 99 out of 100 cases are totally harmless. It's
going to be just fine. We are doing an incredible job.

> *Just stay calm. One day,*
> *It'll be a miracle:*
> *he will disappear.*

Fugue for the First Grandchild

Amy and I are going to be grandparents.
Our daughter called to tell us.
It's their first: he will be an itchy ginger.
But we can't tell anyone yet.

The subject bobs up again:
Amy and I are going to be grandparents,
even as my mind tries to move on.
How can we not tell anyone?

What else is there to talk about?
Our chain is now connected to the future.
Amy and I are going to be grandparents:
we have handed over the magic beans.

I almost get away from it,
but it floats up like the answer
in a magic 8-ball:
Amy and I are going to be grandparents.

Amy and I are going to be grandparents.
I hope you haven't heard:
that means someone we swore to secrecy
broke their oath like we did when we told them.

But the very fact that
Amy and I are going to be grandparents
keeps recurring like the pendulum
in my grandparents' grandfather clock.

We have lost our cool.
Who thought we'd get this old together?
Amy and I are going to be grandparents,
and we can't wait to tell everyone

how grateful we are.
At our age, some of the best are long gone,
along with some of the worst,
but Amy and I are going to be grandparents.

Night Walk

The man I imagine I am
is younger than I am
and better looking.

Women could possibly
still be interested in
the man I imagine I am.

The man I imagine I am
is more agile and strong.
than I am.

Unlike me,
he can still run thirty yards
and catch a football.

Unlike me,
he can safely climb a ladder
to clean out the gutters.

The man I imagine I am
doesn't have to be extra careful
of potholes in the sidewalk.

This is why the man I actually am
blunders into holes,
falls off ladders.

This is why the man I actually am
wears a nightlight on my head
on the late dog walk.

This is why the man I actually am
is constantly trying to remind me:
I'm not the man I imagine I am.

Grandfathers

The two grandfathers were walking
to the beach with their grandson.
A red bird swooped across the path
and landed in the oleanders.
Hugh told six-year-old Brady,
"People say when you see a cardinal,
it's a visit from someone you loved who died."
Brady worries that Hugh and I will die
like BC his dear great-grandmother.

I would tell you that even after I go
and you can't see me anymore,
I will be with you, inside you,
always radiating love,
just like my grandfather,
who is always smiling inside me,
like the glass grate on our old fireplace
on Jenifer Street,
still warm first thing in the morning
no matter how cold it was last night.

I have written it down here
in case I am unable to tell you.

Neruda's Questions

a cento for Susan Laughter Meyers

Have you noticed that autumn
is like a yellow cow?

How do the seasons know
they must change their shirt?

And where are autumn's yellow trousers
left hanging?

Do you feel, in the middle
of autumn, yellow explosions?

Why did the grove undress itself
only to wait for the snow?

Why is it so hard, the sweetness
of the heart of the cherry?

Is it because it must die,
or because it must carry on?

Visits

The story is that each cardinal
is someone you loved who died.
They visit you

when you most need them
or most miss them—
in celebration and despair.

Off our front porch,
cardinals appear every day
in the branches of the loquat tree

in the pin oak, in the live oak,
in the popcorn tree, in the chinaberry,
along the telephone wire,

on the red tin roof
of the apartment next door—
every day, every day.

Wings

a cento from the Book of Psalms

I am a pelican of the wilderness,
a sparrow alone on a rooftop.

I am a night-owl in the desert wind,
tossed up and down like a locust.

My soul escapes as a turtle dove
out of the snare of the fowlers.

Blessed be the Lord for delivering me
from the hands of bloody men.

The birds of the sky nest by the waters,
singing in the branches.

In the shadow of Thy wings,
I take refuge.

I am covered by thy feathers,
and all the trees in the wood are rejoicing.

If, Then

If two red-tailed hawks nest in your tree,
then call your sister and tell her to sell the Studebaker.

If one cloud breaks off and fights the current,
then name your daughter Linoleum.

If a cardinal chases a bluejay from your feeder,
then delete your brother's number from your phone.

If your sister calls back and refuses to sell,
then place three ice cubes around the orchid's stalk.

If your daughter doesn't like her name,
then change your will and give her the Studebaker.

If the bluejay pecks the cardinal in the head,
then put your brother back on speed dial.

If you don't forget the cubes,
then the cloud may float back into formation.

If you can remember where the hawks used to nest,
then the orchid may bloom again next year.

Montego Bay, Jamaica

At this hour the light
is brighter on the water
than in the air,
and all the greens are deepening
into the same color.
The orange flowers
on the African Tulip Tree
and the clumped leaves
of the almond trees
darken, except those
last lit, placed just
where the last light hits.

Then the Tulip Tree
is only a silhouette
against the blackening sky,
and soon it isn't there.

Then the ocean disappears.

Additional Acknowledgments

I am thankful for the patience and support of my dear wife, Amy, and my family and friends for indulging me all these years in my love for poetry. I am particularly lucky and blessed to have connected with Richard Garcia, who has guided and inspired me since I started writing again.

I read these poems during the Sundown Poetry Series at the Piccolo Spoleto Festival in Charleston, South Carolina, in June 2022.

Dewdrop was a featured poem on the *Think* website, 2020.

Emanuel and Ansonborough were performed by Blank Page Poetry at Pure Theater, Charleston, SC, on October 14, 2017.

Ansonborough won the John Bennett Prize, and Touch Me Not won the Gertrude Munzenmaier Prize from the South Carolina Poetry Society, May 2019. If, Then won the Kinloch Rivers Memorial Prize from the Poetry Society of South Carolina in 2016.

Ed is a poet from Baltimore with an M.A. from the Johns Hopkins University Writing Seminars. Ed taught in the English department at the University of Maryland for 15 years and wrote poetry intensely. Then he stepped back from poetry and plunged into the Washington, D.C, federal government arena as a writer, writing trainer, and editor. In his sixties, he bloomed again, churning out poems and working with an amazing group of poets in Charleston, South Carolina. He and his wife, Amy, live in Charleston with their dog, Edie. His first chapbook, *Owl*, was published by SCOP Press.

Milton Keynes UK
Ingram Content Group UK Ltd.
UKHW011033201123
432908UK00005BA/803